1 | Go. Ready. Set.

Go. Ready. Set.

Potential is nothing without pursuit

Doc Murphy

DOC MURPHY MOVEMENTS

GO. READY. SET.

Copyright © 2007-2026 by Doc Murphy

This title is available as an E-book. Visit: www.amazon.com

Request for information should be addressed to:

Doc Murphy, 2220 Coit Rd. Ste 480-123, Plano, Tx. 75075

All Scripture quotations unless otherwise indicated are taken from the Holy Bible. King James Version

All rights reserved. No part of this publication may be reproduced, stored in a retrieval system, or transmitted in any form or by any means-electronic, mechanical, photocopy, recording, or any other-except for brief quotations in printed reviews, without the prior
Permission of the publisher.

Published by Everywhere Publishing 2220 Coit Rd. Ste 480-123, Plano, Tx. 75,075

ISBN: 9781478181620

Printed in the United States of America

Gold Edition

Booking for Doc Murphy:
www.docmurphy.net

E-mail: pastordocmurphy@gmail.com

Instagram @pastordoc | Twitter @pastordoc

Facebook @docmurphymovements

CONTENTS

Preface 5

Introduction 7

CHAPTER ONE: Initiate 14

CHAPTER TWO: God is waiting on you 33

CHAPTER THREE: A Year from Now 39

CHAPTER FOUR: Excuse-ologist 55

CHAPTER FIVE: The Great Resource: TIME 57

CHAPTER SIX: Your Worst Enemy: PROCRASTINATION 62

CHAPTER SEVEN: Faith—The Unstoppable Force 66

CHAPTER EIGHT: Small Things in Big Events 76

CHAPTER NINE: The Audacity to Breakout 82

CHAPTER TEN: Don't Despise the "Going" 91

About the Author 97
Products 98

Preface

I remember running track in high school. It was a lot of fun, but the *rule of track* teaches the: *get ready, get set, and go* mentality. You can't jump the gun, or you'll be disqualified.

Why *Get ready, get set, and go* doesn't work in life.

***Ecclesiastes 11:4* <u>Whoever watches the wind will not plant;</u>** *whoever looks at the clouds will not reap. 5 As you do not know the path of the wind, or how the body is formed in a mother's womb, so you cannot understand the work of God, the Maker of all things. 6 Sow your seed in the morning, and at evening let not your hands be idle, for you do not know which will succeed, whether this or that, or whether both will do equally well.*

In life you must have a different mentality than that of track. You have to learn to **GO, get ready on the way, and when you get there, everything will be set.** You must learn to jump the gun and just go! Most of the time it will never be the right timing (considering your circumstances). Most people are *"wind watchers"* and <u>**they are on the "WAIT" watchers' diet**</u>. They are waiting to see if it's going to be the perfect time before they plant the seed; but like the scriptures says, go ahead and sow and don't allow yourself to get idle. There are certain things you just have to step out on. **Don't wait for things to get better, make things better**. This book is going to teach you how to **overcome the fear of GOING.** I want to help you reach your destiny through the principle of **GO. READY. SET**. Enjoy!

Introduction

*"Now the Lord had said unto Abram, **Get thee out** of thy country, and from thy kindred, and from thy father's house, unto a land that I will show thee…**So Abram departed** as the Lord had spoken unto him…"* (Gen 12:1-4)

Most people have goals—things they want to do and accomplish—but circumstances and fear keep them from pursuing those goals. The fact is that God has given each one of us a purpose and a plan. He has wired us for a unique task that will be a blessing to someone on this earth. A lot of people are running around aimlessly doing things God never intended for them to do. This is because they have not surrendered their lives to Him and asked Him for the plan He has set for them. On the other end, people are living for God but still don't know their purpose, nor will they act on what they believe God has called them to do. Why? Is it from a lack of motivation or self-worth? Are they afraid of what people will think or worried others will stop them? I believe it's all the above.

Most people would like for everything to be perfect before they act. They wait until they have all the money, their home is well, and everything is smooth. But they wake up one morning ten years older, still telling others about these goals that they will accomplish one day. Years pass by, time dwindles, and after all the excuses, there are still no results. Lip service is the most that many people can give. Great dreamers are not hard to find, but great figures of action are! Of the few who actually start the dream God gave them, even fewer finish.

What a feeling it is to be at the start of a new venture! You're ready to rock and roll. You tell everyone. But as soon as the pressure hits and circumstances don't line up with what you envisioned, you are ready to quickly throw in the towel. You toiled all that time with nothing to show for it. But God is using me to tell you this: ***go back out there with a spirit of faith and do it.*** Keep pressing onward, keep speaking the Word, keep advertising, keep ministering, keep being creative, keep researching, keep building, and keep moving forward. Don't stop. Go further! "Anyone can start, but it takes people with guts and determination to finish" (Luke 5:1-9). You must become a self-motivator; your own leader, if you are going to be successful. Fear will rob you, but self-motivation will rob fear. Furthermore, faith (confidence in God's system) will banish fear.

I know it seems like I just jumped right into the lesson, but I did it for a reason. And it is an extremely important reason. You don't have time to waste. It's time for you to get up and do something. **It's time to lose the WAIT!** Go make a difference; go impact your generation for the glory of God. The word *"go"* scares people, because *"go"* takes you out of your COMFORT-zone. ***I'm going to slap the comfort out of your zone!*** *"Go"* takes you to the unknown. The unknown can be intimidating because it is, of course, unknown. But rest assured that God knows what He is doing when He calls you to a place that you've never been before. He will guide you, give you instructions, and get you to the right destination. However, you must take that first step. **Stop trying to figure everything out before you move.** God said go and that's what He meant. **Don't check your budget, check your faith!**

As you go, you will get further

instructions. Don't worry about being embarrassed, because if God has spoken, He will always make you look good. The confusing conundrum about seeing the vision for your life is that God will show you the end, but He seems to forget to show you the beginning and the middle. You see He knows that if He would show us the rough beginning and the rough middle, we wouldn't do it. So instead, He gives us only glimpses of what's to come!

That is exactly what happened to Joseph in Genesis 37-45. God gave him his life's purpose in a dream. God showed him the end of the dream. Joseph didn't know anything about the pit, Potiphar's house, or the prison. But through all his troubles, he stayed faithful to God. God prospered him wherever he was. Can you prosper regardless of where you are? Sure you can if you hold on to your spirit of faith and refuse to allow the enemy to rob you with negative words and discouragement.

When you step out and begin what God has purposed for you to do, you may expect to immediately see the results that you had envisioned. Be patient and keep your expectations high. It may take ten years for that dream to finally come to fruition. Jim Collins of Good to Great once noted that great organizations have a culture of discipline demonstrated by a history of making choices that lead to that greatness. *"Most overnight successes are really about twenty years in the making,"* he said. It took seven years for Sam Walton to open his second store. It took Starbucks thirteen years before they had five stores. It took Joesph 13 years to see his dream come to pass. Whatever your dream may be, if you stay faithful like Joseph, and many others, you WILL see the manifestation of the dream. This is the product of your belief in God. Anyone can quit, but only the most persistent will stand up and keep going.

Those serving Jesus Christ are meant to do great things for the Kingdom of God, because the GREAT ONE abides in them. The Bible says in John 15:5, "without Him (Jesus) we can do nothing." I agree. It is the act of putting our lives in line with His Kingdom that brings greatness into our lives. But we will never accomplish any of that if we don't get up from the many streaming services (binge watching) and go forth to pursue our purpose. The earth belongs to us (Psalm 115:16). It is time for us to make it better with Kingdom righteousness through our God-given assignments. The door is wide open, but we must each make up our own minds to walk through it.

Chapter One
Initiate

What will you initiate today that will affect your tomorrow?

I know you have a vision, a dream, some GOD-GIVEN ideas, but what have you initiated?

You play a major role in God's ultimate mission, but **what have you initiated to secure the success of God's mission?** Are you in your place? Have you discovered your purpose? Have you taken the necessary steps to get started?

The church (Body of Christ) is made up of believers who all have an assignment and everyone's assignment helps the world-wide church fulfill its mission.

15 | Go. Ready. Set.

God has a plan for you, but what plan have you put in place to make sure God's plan will come to pass? God wants you to produce an *ACTION* plan. Don't keep planning to plan. Get out of that mode. Create a plan, but then get to work. Stop trying to get ready and get a *GO* mentality.

People love meetings. They want to plan another meeting so they can discuss ideas *AGAIN*. No, this is the *GO Camp*! We train people to GO. **GO DO something**!

If God's plan for you is to sing around the world, what albums have you produced, what does your website and social media pages look like, and what systems do you have in place for people to hear about you and contact you? This is not luck, it is predictable. I know what's going to happen if I obey God and initiate the proper things. The results are as He said it.

Acts 27:25 So keep up your courage, men, <u>for I have faith in God that it will happen just as he told me</u>

God's will is not automatic. We must work with His plan through proper planning, prayer, preparation, and persistence.

Your faith is proven through how well you prepare for the prophecy.

You're not waiting *(in the sense of doing nothing; waiting for someone to do things for you and open doors for you)* **you're initiating.**

You need to initiate some things this year that will possibly protect you from what's coming in upcoming years. Don't procrastinate on this, initiate immediately.

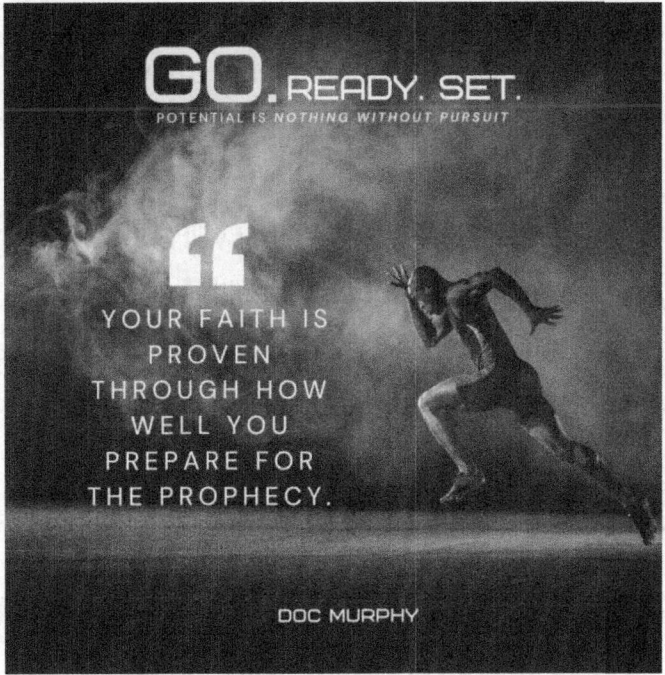

Many people fail because they don't have preventative faith or action. They wait until things happen to them. Did you know there are certain things you can prevent? In order to do this, you must:

- Initiate an **action plan** (not just a vocal and thought plan) that has the greatest possibility of securing your future. Initiate a predictable plan that will work with your faith. Faith is not foolishness and it is not blind. It works with knowledge, prophesies, visions, and Holy Spirit-inspired plans. But you must initiate the process.

What do you have in place that will bring you **pre-determined success**, health, ministry opportunities, business opportunities, and security for the following year?

Why people don't initiate?

They are afraid. Initiating a conversation, initiating sharing their faith with people, initiating a business idea, initiating a ministry assignment, or a new career puts people in a state of fear. Often, people don't get out of the starting blocks because they are afraid. Afraid of failure, persecution, and rejection.

The Holy Spirit will help with this. This is why we must be filled with the Holy Spirit. The Holy Spirit turns you into a Beast! A Beast of Boldness!

2 Timothy 1:7 For this reason I remind you to fan into flame the gift of God, which is in you through the laying on of my hands. **7 <u>For God has not given us a spirit of timidity, but of power, love, and self-control.</u>** *8 So do not be ashamed of the testimony of our Lord, or of me, His prisoner. Instead, join me in suffering for the gospel by the power of God*

Romans 8:15 So **<u>you have not received a spirit that makes you fearful slaves</u>**. *Instead, you received God's Spirit when he adopted you as his own children. Now we call him, "Abba, Father."*

Acts 4:31 After this prayer, the meeting place shook, and **<u>they were all filled with the Holy Spirit. Then they preached the word of God with boldness.</u>**

What do you do when God tells you to initiate something that's completely different from what everyone else is doing?

You must have the audacity (boldness) to break away from people who can't see your vision or try to stop you from doing it.

God told Paul He would deliver him from the people. **Acts 26:16-18**

You must get delivered from people first. This will help you to initiate the things that you must initiate.

What has God asked you to initiate and what are some things that you can start doing now that will help you get to the wealthy place, the healthy place, the ministry place, the restoration place? You can't get to a place until you turn the ignition on and then START driving. Don't sit there hoping everything will turn out alright, be sure of it by initiating the

Word and **<u>putting into practice what you've been taught.</u>**

There is always a walk of faith when you are starting a journey.

Hebrews 11:8 By faith Abraham, when called to go to a place he would later receive as his inheritance, obeyed and went, even though he did not know where he was going

<u>What do you See?</u>

If you're going to walk by faith you will need vision. Vision helps you see. Vision keeps you out of the dark. Vision shows you where to go. Vision helps you initiate, start, go, and walk.

Vision is one of the most important things that should be in your life:

Proverbs 29:18 <u>*New Living Translation*</u>

When people do not accept divine guidance, they run wild. But whoever obeys the law is joyful.

English Standard Version ***Where there is no prophetic vision the people cast off restraint*** but blessed is he who keeps the law.

The vision keeps you within the boundaries of the vision. You don't cast off the restraints. You're not all over the place trying ideas. No, you can SEE what to do and where to go. You're not lost, anxious, or confused when you have a solid God-given vision. No person and No thing can sway you in the opposite direction. ***Vision keeps you on point, focused, solid, and disciplined.***

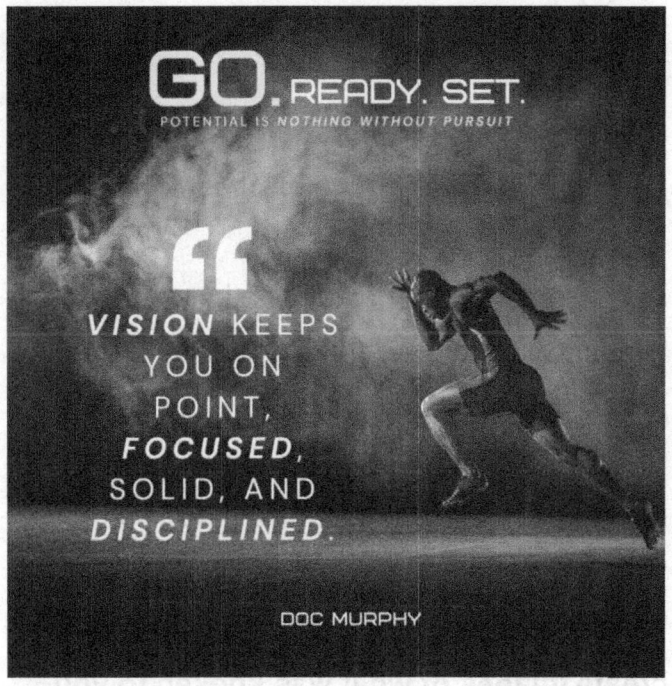

Possibilities can be all around you and you will never see them, and sometimes you will never see what others can see (even though it's obvious). The reason you never see it, is because it was not meant for you to see it like that. You would have never thought of it or seen it. It has always been there, but **God showed it to someone else.** And <u>**what is obvious to you and what is possible to you was shown to you by God for His purpose.**</u> You must recognize it and pursue it.

***Genesis** 12:1-3*

What God did with Abraham was give him a picture and inner image of possibilities.

Becoming a Father of many nations was for him and no one else. **It was Abraham's personal success** and *his Big Picture.*

God needs us to **see what He said.** God's Words are designed to get you to see. His Words create an image. **You are wired to create images of what was spoken to you.**

What do you see?

If you can't see it within, you'll never get it. Mental pictures are designed by God to keep you motivated, obsessed, encouraged, and knowing what's possible for you. *If God said it and if you can see it, then it is possible for you. It may be impossible for others, but it's possible for you.* This is why it is extremely important that you don't copy others just to copy others.

Not one other person was called to be a father of many nations. The Blessing did come on Isaac (Gen 26:4) and Jacob (Gen 28:13-15) but it was originally given to Abraham.

Giant killing was for David. Moses and Joshua parted Seas. The Apostle John saw and wrote the revelation. Only one man made the sun stand still; Joshua. Jesus was Mary's vision and dream. She was the only woman. John the Baptist was the one chosen to baptize Jesus and prepare the way for His coming. Only Nehemiah had the dream to build the wall. Only Samson was anointed to have that kind of strength. You can pray for it all you want and go get a *"prophelie"* for "confirmation", but you are only anointed to do what God **OBVIOUSLY** placed inside of you. God sets you apart, makes you unique, and gives you a Big Picture that's only designed for you!

Today there are still supposed to be only one person doing certain things or just a few people, but this society is so caught up on the wrong definition of success, that basically all everyone does is copy others and casually say, *"God told me"*.

Conferences and seminars are not wrong, but they have almost destroyed our ability to hear from God and be ourselves. We think since *"successful"* people talk like that, act like that, and do that, we should just copy them; even at the expense of changing our personality, voice, and true calling.

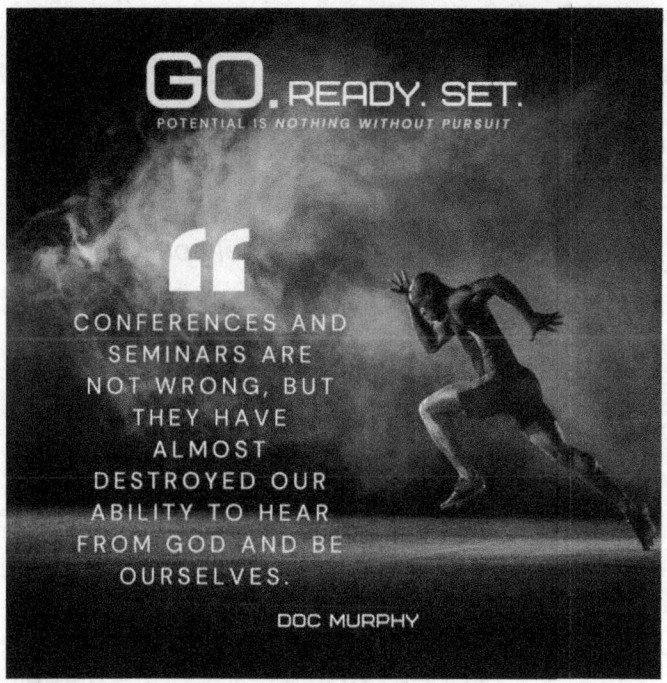

Are you having Vision Problems?

- *Blurred vision (the loss of sharpness of vision and the inability to see fine details)*
- *Blind spots or scotomas (dark "holes" in the vision in which nothing can be seen)*

What's causing your vision to be blurred and what is causes the blind spots?

Your vision may be blurred because of sin, rebellion against spiritual leaders, pride, and listening to unwise and ego-centric people.

Proverbs 4:26 Watch the path of your feet and all your ways will be established. **27 Do not turn to the right nor to the left; Turn your foot from evil.**

*Proverbs 4:**25 (NIV) Let your eyes look straight ahead; fix your gaze directly before you.** 26 Give careful thought to the paths for your feet and be steadfast in all your ways. 27 Do not turn to the right or the left; keep your foot from evil.*

Hebrews 12:1 Therefore, since we are surrounded by such a great cloud of witnesses, let us throw off every encumbrance and the sin that so easily entangles, and let us run with endurance the race set out for us. **2 Let us fix our eyes on Jesus, the pioneer and perfecter of our faith, who for the joy set before Him endured the cross, scorning its**

shame, and sat down at the right hand of the throne of God. *3 Consider Him who endured such hostility from sinners, so that you will not grow weary and lose heart.*

Matthew 13:13 ***This is why I speak to them in parables: 'Though seeing, they do not see; though hearing, they do not hear or understand.'*** *14 In them the prophecy of Isaiah is fulfilled: 'You will be ever hearing but never understanding; you will be ever seeing but never perceiving...*

(This was talking about the religious people who are full of pride)

Stay Focused on what you see

You need Forward Vision

A lesson from Birds

*With **forward**-facing **eyes**, the bald eagle has a wide field of binocular **vision**.*

Vision *is the most important sense for* _birds_*, since good eyesight is essential for safe flight, and this group has a number of adaptations which give visual acuity superior to that of other* _vertebrate_ *groups; a pigeon has been described as "two eyes with wings".*[1] *The avian eye resembles that of a* _reptile_*, with* _ciliary muscles_ *that can change the shape of the* _lens_ *rapidly and to a greater extent than in the* _mammals_*. Birds have the largest eyes relative to their size in the animal kingdom, and movement is consequently limited within the eye's bony socket. In addition to the two eyelids usually found in vertebrates, it is protected by a third transparent movable membrane. The eye's internal anatomy is similar to that of other vertebrates, but has a structure, the* _pecten oculi_*, unique to birds.*

Some bird groups have specific modifications to their visual system linked to their way of life. _Birds of prey_ *have a very high density of receptors and other adaptations that maximize visual acuity. The placement of their eyes gives them **good binocular vision** enabling* *accurate judgement of distances. <u>Nocturnal</u> species have tubular eyes, low numbers of colour detectors, but a high density of rod cells which function well in poor light. <u>Terns</u>, <u>gulls</u> and <u>albatrosses</u> are amongst the <u>seabirds</u> which have red or yellow <u>oil droplets</u> in the color receptors to improve distance vision especially in hazy conditions.*

As we can see, birds purposely have great vision. We need to have the kind of spiritual eyes that give us a good binocular vision that will enable us to accurately judge our future properly.

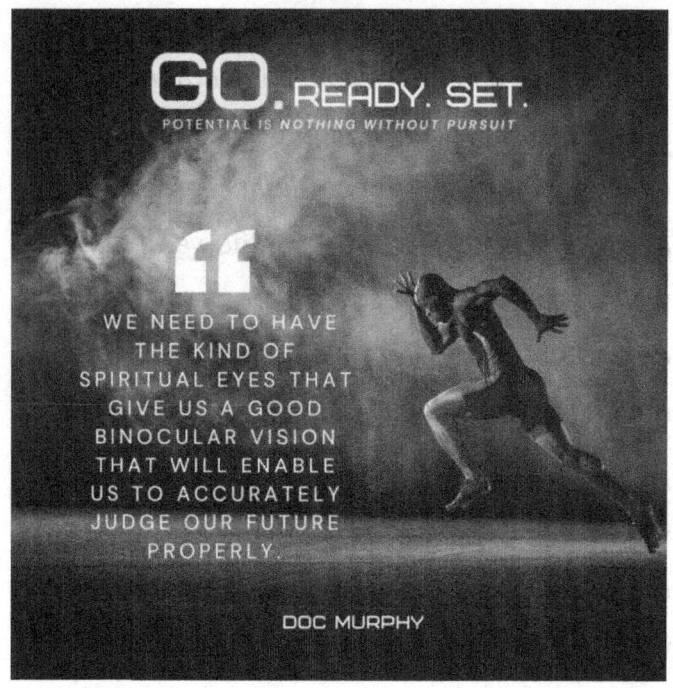

When you're focused like Paul was, you will be able to say:

Acts 26:19 "So then, King Agrippa, **_I was not disobedient to the vision from heaven._**

Chapter Two
God Is Waiting on You, So
LOSE THE WAIT!

It is amazing how many people use the excuse that they are waiting on God when ***it is God who is waiting on them.*** People are still praying about what God already told them to do, going to revival after revival trying to hear another confirmation from the prophet and manipulating God to speak. **<u>God is not going to speak to you or give you another confirmation until you learn to obey Him on what He already told you</u>**. This waiting stems from fear and insecurity. You don't pray about walking on the water if Jesus has already said, "Come." You just go and trust that everything else will be set.

Moses and Gideon had problems trusting the plan God had for them. They wanted God to keep showing signs, repeat His orders, and send out further confirmation

(Exodus 3:22 & 4:1-3, Judges 6:11-40). They were caught up in their own limitations and insecurities. **They were too busy worrying about what they thought of themselves rather than what God thought of them**.

Although God did give them signs, their purpose wasn't fulfilled **until they obeyed God**.

<u>Don't ever get trapped in waiting for God to give you a steady stream of signs before you are convinced to believe what He has called you to do.</u> The longer you wait, the less you'll be convinced. Satan loves nothing more than for us to wait, claiming that we are waiting on God. Waiting on God for what? He has already spoken. The next step is to trust Him (Psalms 62:8). You certainly may not be used to that type of aggressive faith, but God is, and He knows what's ahead of you. He knows every enemy, every obstacle, and every victory. Just move in faith; trust that God knows best and that He will lead you to your

perfect destiny. So, remember, you're not waiting on God. He is waiting on you to take the step.

Fear will rob you.

The fear of rejection, the fear of looking ridiculous because you don't have everything you need to LOOK successful, the feeling of embarrassment, the fear of wondering what others think about your SMALL beginning—all these fears rob us of pursuing our goal. But you have to be like Joshua and Caleb and take on a *Spirit of Faith* that says, *"We're not grasshoppers, but champions in God"* (Numbers 13:30 & 14:24). "If God be for us, He is more than the world against us." You must step out into unknown territory and trust that God will lead. He will pay for it. He will handle your adversaries. He will make a WAY (Isaiah 43:19). God is the King of the unknown because it is not unknown to Him; it's just unknown to you! Trust Him, my friend, and get to MOVING! You don't have to understand everything. You don't have to get every detail. You don't have to feel goose bumps. You don't have to hear another testimony from a celebrity preacher. Just GO and leave the rest to God. He's WISE!

God Didn't Show Everything!

Isn't it amazing that God only shows you the "successful you"—the end of the story? He never seems to show you the start or the middle of your destinies. That's why the dream is so exciting, and you want to tell everyone. It wouldn't be so exciting if God showed you how many people would come against you, how the money wouldn't be there, and how you would have to fast and pray and believe for a miracle to pay for it. Nor would it be exciting if he showed you how the enemy would try to stop you with sickness, how your own family would come against you, how you would get laughed at and called an idiot, and how you would sit around wondering *"did God really call me to do this, because it doesn't seem like it's working."*

No, God shows the exciting, happy parts of the dream. After we share it with everyone, then we realize, "Hey I don't have any money for this, any support, any members, any clients, or any CREDIT" (or worse, bad credit). That's when fear kicks in and we wonder, *"Did God really speak this to me? Did I miss something?"* Then you start talking about everything that's WRONG with you, instead of what's right with you, what's right with God and His WORD.

God's Dream is bigger than you!

My friend, every dream God gives is specific just for you and sometimes it's bigger than your bank account, your logic, your reasoning, or your support. God wants you to trust Him, know His power, learn to lead yourself, and walk by faith. You must change your attitude by changing the way you think about yourself and the way you talk about yourself. Start thinking the thoughts of God and speaking the Words of God over your life.

If God spoke to you, then you have everything it takes to get the job done. You must believe that, or you'll never move. You will sit there for thirty more years waiting on God. Believe in God, believe His spoken and written Word, and believe in your born-again self. Do the impossible and make a liar out of the devil, "for all things are possible with God" (Mark 10:27)!

What is your GOD-GIVEN dream?

_____

_____

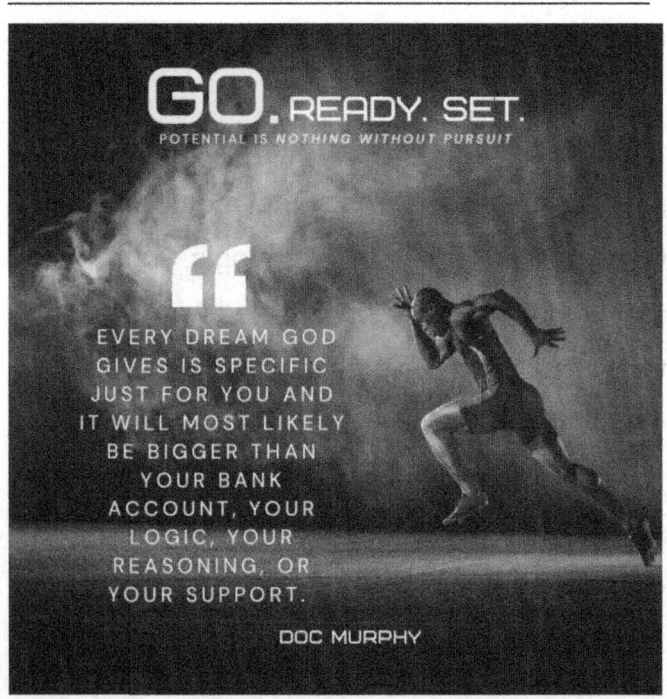

Chapter Three
A Year from Now You Will Wish You Had Started!

A year from now, you will wish you had started! That's a powerful statement, and it shouldn't be taken lightly. Don't delay—get started today! **Now** is all you have. Too many people waste time pondering over the dream instead of starting the dream. You'll never start until you start. You'll never move until you move. Stop procrastinating and get up and start. Each second you wait, you're getting older, you're losing time, and you're getting further and further behind. You must eliminate the things that are holding you back. Recognize those dream killers, those things or people that keep you paralyzed. You must get to the root of the thing that's keeping you from starting. Is it fear? One day you will look up, and have regrets, wishing about the thing you most wanted to do but never pursued.

By this time next year, will you have accomplished your goals? Will you be happy that you started NOW? Or will you regret that you let something, yourself, or someone hold you back AGAIN? My friend, there are some people you may not be able to take along on the journey. Let them go. Your dream is too important for you to sit around with someone who is keeping you from achieving it and wasting your time!

Getting ready on the way is an ART!

You must learn the art of getting ready on the way. Yes, *you're wasting too much time trying to get ready. Instead, get ready while you're running. Move forward and go after the vision God has given you*. You'll never know if it will work if you don't do it. Don't just try it. Do it. People that try stuff never complete STUFF! Trying always leaves you with some escape and it is simply a form of doubt. You don't try to get married. You don't say, "I'll try." You say, "I DO!" You don't try to accomplish your dream; you accomplish it regardless of the pitfalls that come your way. The Bible didn't say, *"The just should try to live by faith,"* it said, *"the just shall live by faith"* (Romans 1:17). God is about doing, pursuing, and going; not trying, wishing, and procrastinating.

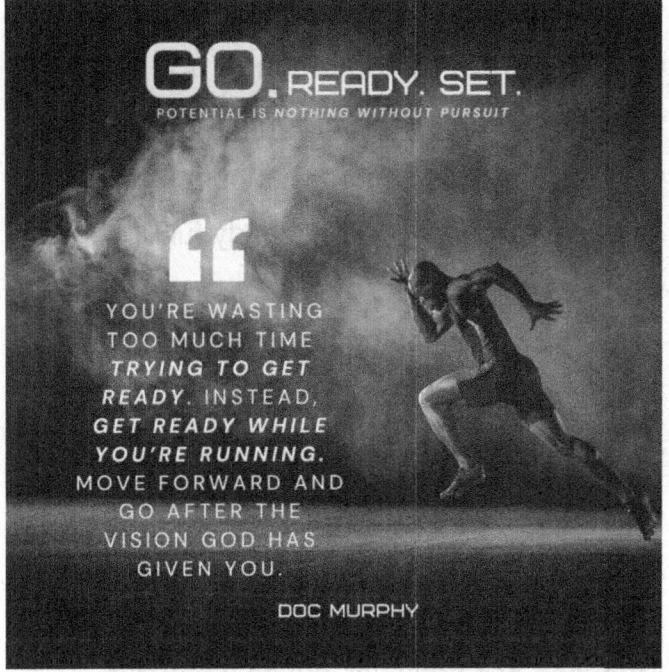

The grave is full of untapped potential— books, dreams, inventions, companies, authors, teachers, and great ministries that never got started. Every day people are dying without accomplishing their purpose, and the dream that God gave them gets buried with them, never to be realized. This is because they didn't go after it. They spent too much time worrying about things that didn't matter. Never waste time with wasted time!

Potential is nothing if you don't do what you have the potential to do. In other words, **_potential is nothing without pursuit_**. One day, my wife shared with our church that I don't have potential—I'm already fulfilling what God has called me to do!

Do you want people to always say that you have the potential to do something? You would rather hear them say, "*Wow, that person is making a difference in the world. That person has a great company or a great ministry. They are really **_DOING_** a great job.*" Everyone has potential, but so what! It's nothing without action! Abraham had potential to be a father of many nations, but he had to start his relationship with Sarah and trust that God would bless them in order to begin the process! Samson had potential to destroy the Philistines, but he had to go FIGHT! He didn't sit around and ponder and get happy about what people were saying about him. No, he had to *"get off the couch"* and go fight. David had great potential to kill Goliath, but he had to shoot his slingshot. The important thing to note about David is that his slingshot was already in his hand. He didn't use someone else's weapon. As ridiculous as it may have seemed, he believed that he could kill the giant with a slingshot. He knew that God was on his side, and God is bigger than any giant. He thought, "God can use what I have and I'm getting ready to cut off Goliath's head." He killed a lion and a bear before that, so the giant was nothing to him. My friend, when you start, you may start with something ridiculous, something that you already have, but use it anyway, and don't get embarrassed. God will take your small resources. He'll take what you have if you are willing to start. He will turn it into a tremendous resource for you. It will in turn be a blessing to others.

I remember when God called me to preach. I was 19 years old. I preached my first sermon at my home church and got a few more engagements after that. I knew God called me to preach and win souls for Him. So, I didn't wait for a Sunday or Wednesday to preach to those who had already been reached. I went to the streets and declared the gospel of Jesus Christ! I had a tape recorder, and I would record myself preaching. Then I would make copies and put them in people's mailboxes (at that time I didn't know that was illegal)! The point is, I didn't wait. God said preach! I would go into neighborhoods and preach to people. I would preach in churches when I **wasn't** invited to preach (of course that didn't go over so well). When God tells you to do something, He means now! Of course, there are some things God wants us to have patience with and wait on His timing, but we must put in the effort He is calling us to put forth. My point is that so many people use the excuse that they are waiting on God, praying for the timing. But really, they are afraid—afraid of rejection, wondering if anyone is going to like them.

I grew fast as a minister. God blessed my efforts. The reason is I was active in my early years. Sure, there were a lot of things I didn't know, but what I did know I taught. I put it out in full confidence and faith, and God helped me with the rest.

When God called me to do apostolic work (church planting) I had nothing. I had no money, no members, and no prospects (other than five other friends and family—that's about it). All I had was a dream, a vision, and my potential *(true potential comes from the written Word of God and God's anointing (calling) on your life)*. I had no training in ministry. I didn't know anything about being an apostle/pastor/teacher. Should I have waited until everything was perfect, content just to talk about the potential I had for ministry? Should I have spent four years in seminary school, waiting for a degree to tell me I could plant a church movement? Should I have worried that people would only take me seriously if I had a certificate? Should I have feared that I was going into unknown territory? Should I have given up when people laughed and said I was not called to do it (sure enough they did)? Should I have tried to talk God out of it because I didn't have any money or supporters? Should I have waited until I could get a *"church building"*? Should I have doubted God even after God had already spoken? You know what I did—a little 19-year-old lad? That's correct! I started without any money, without a building, with 4 members, without a musician, without a choir, without a secretary, without a computer, without a quality suit, and without a degree or manual (no Apostolic Work 101, even though I needed a book or something).

I started in one of the member's home. I was the administrator and almost everything in between. I learned the keyboard so we could have music (It sounded horrible). I taught a couple of people how to play the drums so we could have some kind of beat. Instead of bus ministry, we had our cars (we walked through the streets to win people for Jesus and get them to come to the house). We had ushers in that house (the kids were the ushers). One time we had a three' o'clock program (I learned that from my Baptist friends) and invited other churches to that small living room. Hey, we were a church, so we were acting like it (acting like the traditional church we came out of…ha). I wasn't embarrassed (I'm sure the others were, they just never admitted it). All I knew is God said plant a church, so that's what we did. Of course, it wasn't a masterpiece, but I was learning. As I stepped out, God began to show me things. He taught me how to teach, how to care for the sheep, how to become outwardly focused, how to delegate and train leadership, how to make disciples, and how to build a healthy church. I learned on the way. I didn't wait until everything was perfect. I'm glad I started back then (31 years ago) or I wouldn't be where I am today. I'm still learning and developing. I'm grateful for my spiritual mentors who have played a huge role in my spiritual and leadership development. Through their leadership and teachings, we have been able to see parts of our vision come to reality.

I'm glad I started then, so I wouldn't be regretting it now! God has called us to launch a church movement called The Everywhere Network and we have been obedient to that and have planted many churches around the nation. We have a vision to have a church in every city of the United States and beyond! We are also working on many businesses, health, entertainment, fashion, musical, sports, technological, Real Estate, and educational *Ventures*.

It has been a major step of faith, and we will continue to humble ourselves and be obedient unto death. Favor, resources, and wisdom are coming as a result of our actions. God gives you more on the way than what you started with. A new venture never seems like the right timing, and people will make sure they

49 | G o . R e a d y . S e t .

express their doubts through their words or actions. But you must become a person who will obey amid adversity! We are off the launching pad and God is being glorified through it all!

A lady prophesied to me when I was 16 years old. She told me that God called me to also be a minister of music. She said I would write and produce songs. At that time, I didn't know how to write songs, I couldn't play the keyboard (I played the drums), and I didn't know the first thing about producing music. I wasn't even born again when she spoke that into my life. Well, that next year I did get born again, and I immediately remembered the prophecy. While I was walking to the store one night, my first song came to me. I ran home, wrote it down, and dated it. It was exciting. From that point on, I would get inspired and write songs. I didn't go to a songwriting coach; God gave me the inspiration. I've now written hundreds of songs—so many that I stopped counting. I've produced multiple albums and

EP projects, and I can finally play the keyboard a bit. I taught myself how to play. I didn't wait to start. I started and used what I had (which was really nothing). Even though it sounded horrible when I first started playing in church gatherings, I pretended like it was great!

In 1997 I did my first EP. But...that EP project was made using a karaoke machine. I couldn't afford studio time. I played on my keyboard, and my wife sang two songs that I wrote. I made labels for the cassettes, packaged them, and put them in a store in my hometown. And they sold out! People thought we had recorded in a studio. Once again, I started with what I had and pushed forward. That was just training ground. I wasn't embarrassed. All I knew is God said I would produce albums, so I wanted to produce some albums. We had no money, no studio equipment, no professional musicians, and no singers. But we had inspiration from God, a karaoke machine, one microphone, a toy-sounding keyboard, a vocalist, and two songs.

That was good enough for me to get started. How about you? We now have a successful independent record label called Creative Apostle Everywhere.

Back in the 90's God called me to the world of business. I call it Kingdompreneurship. As you can probably guess, I had no experience. I had never read a book on business structure, I didn't have much money to invest, and I didn't have a business coach to advise me. I just got out there and launched all kinds of businesses. I never made huge profits in any of them, but I wasn't afraid to make something happen. I used my apartment number as a suite number on my letterheads. I used an eight hundred number voicemail, and then I used the pay phone to call clients back (we didn't have a home phone). I would spend all our money investing in random ventures. Yes, I was making huge mistakes, and yes, my wife was mad! But all of that was Business School 101 for me. I learned a lot. Now I can look back and laugh at all the stories but let me tell you—my wife was not laughing at the time. We were losing cars and getting evicted. We survived on a steady diet of rice, and I had to pawn almost everything. I used to wash my suits in the washer and iron them myself because I couldn't afford dry cleaning. **Warning: Don't try this at home!**

Over the years we gained wisdom from God and mentors and have been successful in business. I've helped many people launch businesses and consult them in their marketing and sales endeavors. Now as part of my ministry, I teach business courses and I lead business seminars. Our Coaching Business is called Widman University Everywhere.

I write books, produce music, develop leaders and business owners, and I run a fantastic apostolic ministry. The point is that I started somewhere. I made some bad choices (I'm not telling you to just go out there and be unwise, making bad decisions), but I started and gained valuable knowledge and wisdom along the way. I wasn't going to wait until it got better or until the timing seemed perfect. If you want a better life, go out there and create it. Don't sit around another minute with enormous potential. **Start, because a year from now, you will be wishing you had started.**

3 WAYS TO GET STARTED & ACCOMPLISH YOUR GOAL IN A YEAR

1. Start Small, Stay Consistent.

Don't chase *big starts*; chase *daily steps*. Consistency will take you places talent and talk never will.

2. Break It into Quarters.

Think in 90-day wins. Every 3 months, measure your progress, adjust your plan, and push harder. Small sprints create big breakthroughs.

3. Partner with People who are doing their purpose.

Don't do it alone. Get around people who

stretch your faith, challenge your focus, and won't let you settle for average.

Chapter Four
Excuse-ologist

I am shocked by the multitude of excuses I hear from people concerning their lives. "I don't know how." "I don't know where to start." "We grew up on the wrong side of the tracks." "I am black, and they are holding me back." "I am a woman, and they are discriminating." "They told me I wouldn't amount to anything." "Nobody likes my idea." "I'm afraid." "I don't think it will work." "They told me I was crazy." "I need money." "I wish someone would help." "I had a bad childhood." "I have a special problem." "My leg hurts." "I'll start once I catch up on all the bills." What are your excuses? *Like Peter Daniels says, "Are you an excuse-ologist"?* **Do you major in excuses? It's easy to find an excuse for not doing something.** People who make excuses are wimps. They allow their circumstances to whip them. Fear of rejection and fear of failure are keeping people in bondage. My friend, you will never pursue your purpose until you get rid of all the excuses. I'll help you out: **You're not the only one who had struggles in life.** Most successful people had it rough, too. But they rid themselves of the excuses and went out and did something to improve their lives. An excuse is your worst enemy. It helps you to procrastinate. <u>**An excuse helps you to hide behind fear. It's a way to make you feel better about not accomplishing your goals and dreams.**</u> God hates excuses. When King Saul sinned, he immediately made an excuse for why he did it instead of confessing he was wrong. God would have appreciated Saul if he would have just simply confessed and repented, but he had to make up an excuse first. He lost the kingdom because of an excuse. Yes, it was sin, but he immediately went into excuse mode (I Samuel 15:1-23). If you want to hold on to your assignment, stop making excuses and pursue the dream with integrity.

Chapter Five
The Great Resource: TIME

God created time for us. He gave us time as a resource to utilize and manage. If you don't learn to manage your time, you will waste it. If you waste time, you lose in life. Most people don't appreciate time; they just let it slip by them day after day. They let others waste their time. They waste time doing things that don't matter. The priorities that should take precedence are usually not the highest priorities for most people. ***Instead, there is a spirit of procrastination, goofing off, and daydreaming that takes over people's lives.*** They are busybodies who are in other people's business instead of taking care of their own business. They think they have all the TIME in the world to laze around. There is nothing wrong with playing, relaxing, sleeping, doing a hobby, or reading a book. And there is certainly nothing wrong with studying the Bible, spending time with God in prayer, or going to

Church gatherings. But how much time are we going to spend sleeping and playing around? Some people sleep so long that they are too tired to do anything after they wake up! There must be time management in your life.

I teach people to accomplish the things that matters the most. **Priorities are supposed to be first.** Create a time management schedule for each day (a list of things to do for the day) and accomplish the things on that list each day. Don't allow the little things to distract you and get you off course of what you are supposed to be doing. Can you find someone else to do the responsibilities that you really shouldn't be doing? That's called leadership. Every leader needs to learn the art of delegation. Everyone is a leader, and the first person you should lead is YOU. You must be able to lead yourself and make sure YOU accomplish the important things and utilize the time you have. <u>**It's easy to get caught up in a conversation that will waste your time, but you can't**</u>

allow it. Learn to speak up and simply say, *"I have to get back to what I was doing."* The clock is ticking, my friend. If you keep wasting time you will be depressed by what you did not accomplish.

Wake Yourself Up!

No one is going to wake you up; no one is going to babysit you; and no one is going to feel sorry for you because you had a bad childhood. Often people waste so much time telling everyone about their past experiences that they can't pursue things in their present life. I am sorry about whatever may have happened, but now that it's over, it's time to get past it with the help of God, His Word, and a good community of godly friends. Go use your time to do something great in this world for Jesus. **Stop being a baby, waiting on everyone to help you.** Grow up and help someone else get on their feet. Mature people learn to *"get over themselves"* and use their time to do some good for others. We all go through tough times in life, but we can achieve victory through the Word and through our FAITH! (I John 5:4-5)

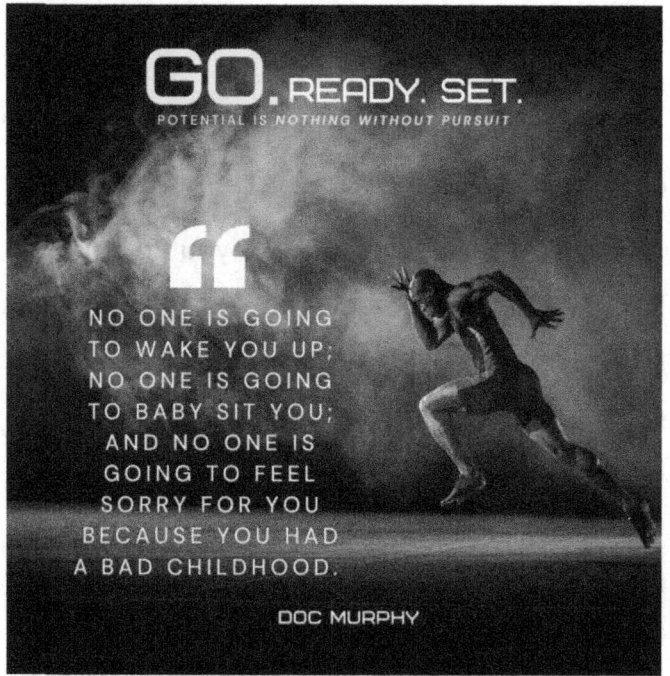

The wealthy know that time is their most valuable asset. Others let it pass, not realizing that someone else is stealing time from them. The average person thinks money is the most valuable thing. The wealthy say, *"I can get more money, but I can never get more time."* You can replace nearly anything in life except for time. It is the only limited resource you have. The wealthy know this and will never let you steal their time.

Just think, you could get others to clean your house and mow your lawn, and you could use that time to make thousands of dollars like the rich do. Most people wouldn't do it, because they have a *middle-class* mentality. They figure that if they had extra money to pay for chores, they should give that money to the poor. **But you could give more money to the poor if you had more time to make more money.**

Time is on your side. But you must use it, manage it, and work with it if it is going to benefit you. Start today by making a to-do list for each day. You will be amazed at how much you will accomplish. Remember that time is your most valuable resource.

Chapter Six
Your Worst Enemy:
PROCRASTINATION

Have you ever gone into to the office with tons of things to do, only to find yourself sitting around and looking into the sky once you are there? Have you ever been excited about a project but never got started? Have you ever said you were going to do something, yet you never got around to it? Procrastination has taken over. You would be further along in life if you wouldn't procrastinate. Just do it! Let me say it again, "Just do it!"

The longer you procrastinate, the more time you waste. There is something in all of us that wants to say, *"I'll get to it later." "Oh, I'll start tomorrow." "I'll do it next week, I got it, and I'll do it."* The fact is you never get to it. It will still be unfinished, because if you procrastinate today, you will also procrastinate tomorrow. It's a mentality that must be broken.

You must crank your engine and motivate yourself to get on it NOW! You must learn the principle of NOW. NOW is powerful. *"I'm going to do it now."* Even one second of waiting will make you procrastinate. Come on and practice it. Say, *"I'll do it NOW!"* Some of you said to yourselves that you'd do it after you read the rest of this chapter! Do it now!

Procrastination is laziness. It makes you lazy. The more you procrastinate, the more you don't want to do it. The longer it takes, the lazier you will feel. Have you ever said, *"Now I don't feel like doing it"?* You see if you had done it when you felt like it, you would've gotten it out of the way. You also need to understand that you should do the right thing because it's the right thing to do. This has nothing to do with feelings. Do it whether you feel like it or not!

Procrastinators are never successful in life. Why? It is because success is an attainment, or an accomplishment of a goal.

Procrastinators don't accomplish goals, so therefore they are not successful.

Procrastinators let opportunities pass them by. They see windows of opportunities, yet they never dive into them because they figure those same opportunities will be there tomorrow. They find out quickly that some opportunities are just passing by. Learn to move NOW. Learn to dive into it NOW while you know the opportunity is available. Practice by doing the important things around your house, your office, your church, with God, and with your family NOW! Stop putting things off. Lead yourself and motivate yourself to *"Just do it!"*

4 WAYS TO STOP PROCRASTINATING

1. Stop Waiting on Perfect Conditions.
There will never be a perfect time—only *God's time*. MOVE when He says GO.

2. Kill the Excuses.
Excuses are dream-killers dressed up as logic.

Stop explaining why you *can't* and start declaring what you *will*.

3. Set a Deadline.
If God gave you the vision, set the clock. Write the goal, attach a date, and let Heaven hold you accountable.

4. Build Momentum Fast.
Do one small thing immediately. One call, one step, one post, one move. Momentum breaks hesitation every time.

Chapter Seven
Faith—The Unstoppable Force

There is no greater force than faith (confidence in God and His Word) (Hebrews 11:1 & 11:6, Romans 1:17). Faith will get you moving. ***It is the unstoppable force that will put action to your words.*** What you need is action in your life, and faith is what will get your feet moving. **<u>Faith will make you jump the gun.</u>** You already heard God speak to you. You're not waiting for the approval or affirmation of others. You're not moving to the sound of their "gun". Since you've heard God, you just need to go, because you'll never be ready (there will never be a perfect time). And when you go, you'll be set. Learn to get ready on the way. You may not have all the information or resources, but you do have a Word from God, a purpose, and a designed destiny. So, you better get to moving.

Faith without works (the corresponding action to what God has spoken) is DEAD (James 2:17-18). Faith is dead if it has no action. People who sit on their haunches saying they are waiting on God by faith are not in faith. They are just talking a good game. They never get in the game. They are waiting for their circumstances to get better. They are **trying to get ready and set.** They are still in the blocks of life, waiting for someone to fire the gun so they can finally move when someone else says they should.

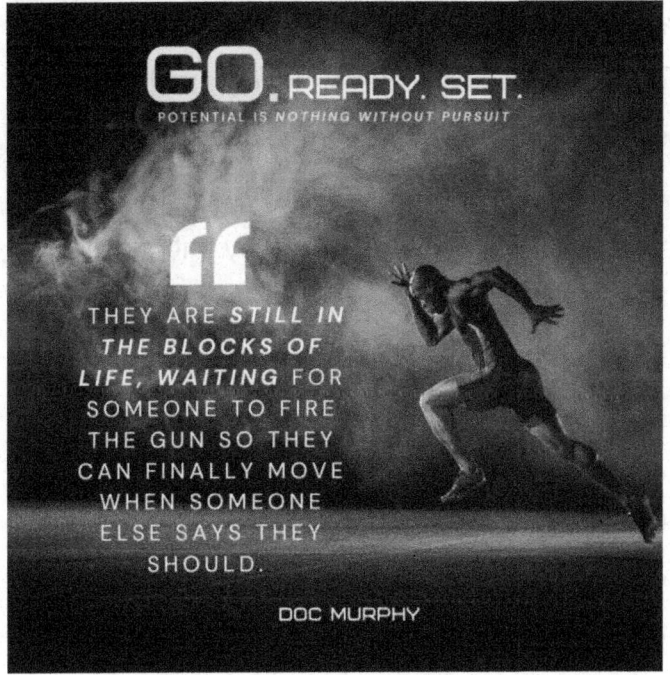

I'm not talking about being rebellious to your spiritual father or mother. You are to obey those who have the rule over you. Many times, it is your pastor who God is talking through. Faith moves to God's say-so, faith jumps the gun, faith says "God has spoken, and it's time to go." "I'll get ready on the way, and when I get there everything will be set." So, it's really **GO, READY, SET!!**

Faith is not foolishness

Faith is not foolishness. You don't move out if God didn't speak to you. You don't just go out there and make a move based on selfish ambition. You don't quit your job (trying to be spiritual) and lose everything, just to say you are living by faith. Living by faith is living by every WORD that comes out of God's mouth (Matthew 4:4). Did God tell you to give away your furniture, your car, or your house? Are you doing things because you saw your favorite faith preacher do them? Are you just copying others or are you really listening for the voice of God?

This book is not about you going out here and being STUPID. I am not calling it **GO BE STUPID.** This is a book aimed at motivating you to step out and pursue the dream, the vision, the Word, and the purpose that you know God has given you. It's about moving now and not wasting time. It's not about making up things that will still cause you to lose in life just for the sake of being able to say that you did something.

<u>**You must have an arrow in your hand and a target to throw it at**</u>. You can't live life aimlessly, hoping (wishing) something will happen. That's not faith. Faith is solid, and faith is intelligent. Faith will cause you to make wise decisions and will point you at a specific destination, knowing you will win in the end. Faith steps out on a solid vision (Habakkuk 2:1-4). Without a vision you will perish, you will live wildly, you will live with no direction or boundaries (Proverbs 29:18). **<u>Faith is not at work in your life if it has no direction</u>** (Acts 27:1-26). God spoke to Abraham and told him

to go to a place, but he also told him what the place was once he stepped out (Genesis 12:1-5). Faith is not going to keep you in the dark or the unknown. It may start out unknown, but God will enlighten you. **_God will always speak to you, giving you direction when you go and obey._**

There are so many people running around who never have a clue what their true purpose is. They are just out there saying they are living by faith, but at the same time they are always saying, "I don't know what to do." "Where is guidance going to come from?" "I wish God would speak to me."

He will speak to you when you are in His will rather than your own (Ephesians 5:17). It's easy to figure out the difference: **when God is not giving you direction about where to go next or what to do next, then you are doing what you made up**. God is not obligated to bless what you've birthed. And don't be deceived—everything that seems to be working is not always God. Anyone can MAKE something happen with enough hard work, but they will never be fulfilled if it is not God's will (Psalms 37:7).

Suffer and Sacrifice

There are two words you need to understand: suffer and sacrifice. Don't make your family suffer because you chose to do something that God didn't tell you to do (often out of bad motives and ignorance). That's suffering for no reason. If you are doing that, stop now, and go get a job or start a simple business to get your family back on their feet. Now if God told you to jump the gun and go, explain to your family that there will be some level of sacrifice, and ask them to support you in it. Then they will see the hand of God working on your behalf as you step out onto the waters of faith. Our minds must be renewed in this area of faith.

So many believers have made genuine faith walkers look bad with their foolish, so-called-faith lifestyle. They are mistaken that living by faith means to give away all their possessions, quit their jobs, and live on the streets with their kids! And they say that God told them to live that way. My question is: if God told them to do it, why does everyone around them suffer trying to help them? Why are they worrying about their situation if it is God's will? Don't cry or worry if you believe God said it. Shouldn't you be trusting God and rejoicing?

Those people go get jobs as soon as they say God told them to quit their jobs! They live off government assistance. They know it's a bunch of CRAP! Don't ever let someone put you under pressure to help them when they do stupid things like that. Let them suffer, because God may not want you to give to them. I've seen people go broke trying to help others who do those things.

When God speaks to you, other people around you should benefit, not suffer trying to help you. When God speaks to you, it's smooth, even when it's rough if you're following His lead. When God speaks to you, it's sweatless, because God always supplies your need according to His riches (Philippians 4:19, Psalms 23:1).

    I must warn everyone: **don't lie on God!** Too many people are lying about what God has told them, saying, "God said this; God said that." Be careful about what you say God said. Some people can hardly hear what I say, so I doubt that they are hearing God!

    Back to faith: Satan hates a faith walker, someone who is so confident in God that they will obey any Word that God says to them. Abraham, our "father of faith," believed and obeyed God no matter what he was asked to do. It was accounted unto him for righteousness (Romans 4:3 & 17-22). God was able to use Abraham mightily because he didn't wait to get ready while sitting in the blocks of life. He heard God and "Abraham went." Abraham got ready on the way, and when he got there everything was set. When God asked Abraham to sacrifice his son, Abraham went. He obeyed, because He trusted God. Of course, he didn't understand what or why, but he obeyed. When Abraham put his arm up to kill his son, God stopped him and told him to hold back his hand. There was a ram in the bush. In other words, Abraham didn't sit there; questing God for years, wondering why God would tell him to do that. He didn't pray about what God had already told him. He didn't get into fear, but he went and got ready on the way. And when he got there, it was all set—a ram in the bush for the sacrifice (Genesis 22:1-14).

Faith doesn't mean you always understand what you are doing or what God says, but faith says, "I will obey God no matter what, because **_He always has everything set on the other end of my obedience._**"

75 | Go. Ready. Set.

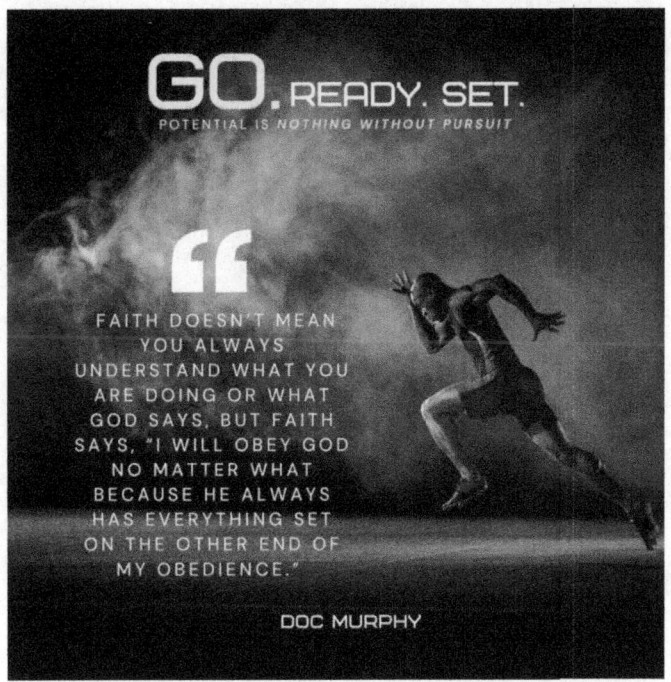

Faith doesn't wait; it moves. But if faith is waiting, it is still active. Our waiting is not a passive waiting; it is an active waiting. Faith talks that which it always believes. Faith is not afraid. It will step right into the purpose, ready for an adventure in God. Stay in faith. Keep the faith switch on and do what God has called you to do. **<u>No wavering, no wondering, and no waiting (James 1:6).</u>**

Not ready set go but go ready set. Jump the gun and move on to greater success today!

Chapter Eight
SMALL THINGS IN BIG EVENTS

"And Elijah said unto Ahab, Get thee up, eat and drink; for there is a sound of abundance of rain. So Ahab went up to eat and to drink. And Elijah went up to the top of Carmel; and he cast himself down upon the earth, and put his face between his knees, And said to his servant, Go up now, look toward the sea. And he went up, and looked, and said, There is nothing. And he said, Go again seven times. And it came to pass at the seventh time, that he said, Behold, there ariseth a little cloud out of the sea, like a man's hand. And he said, Go up, say unto Ahab, Prepare thy chariot, and get thee down, that the rain stop thee not. And it came to pass in the mean-while, that the heaven was black with clouds and wind, and there was a great rain. And Ahab rode, and went to Jezreel."

Go. Ready. Set.

I Kings 18: 41-45

Elijah heard a sound from something small. Until you can hear a sound from the small things, until you can see potential in the small things, until you can be encouraged in the small things, God will never entrust you with BIG clouds. You need to be able to hear sounds that no one else hears. You need to be able to see visions that no one else can see. You need to be able to prophesy to your own destiny!

I will study and prepare, and my opportunity will come. - Abraham Lincoln

We need to get ready and be prepared for the big events in our lives. God intends to use what you have in big events. It will bring an enormous amount of significance to your life. You don't need a lot. You simply need to give what you have to Jesus and have faith in Him.

Small things in big events will make people influential. God knows how to get you to your BIG event. But you must be ready, proven, and have the audacity to use what seems to be insignificant in the big event.

David used a sling shot and rocks in his big event. Moses used a rod in his big event and parted the red sea. Elijah used his faith in a big event. Joseph used his ability to lead and interpret dreams in his big event. A little boy brought his lunch to a big event and it fed over 5,000 people. Rahab used her house in a big event. Peter preached a powerful sermon in a big event and helped launch the first New Testament Church. God gave him a platform because he was prepared. **He was not perfect, but he was prepared.** The widow woman used a morsel of bread in her big event. The widow woman used a pot of oil in her big event. Samson used a jawbone of a donkey in a big event and killed one thousand Philistines. Joshua used his leadership skills and a shout in a big event. These people are being talked about over and over and over, because they decided to have faith in God and use what they had in big events.

What will get you to the Big Event?

You must know what's in your hands.

Work with what's in your hands. Sometimes God will use what you have now to get you to where He really wants you to be. God's purpose for David was to be King, not a giant slayer. But he had to slay giants, kill bears and lions to help get him to the perfect will of God. Joseph's purpose was not to interpret dreams, it was to become the second man in charge of Egypt and save the world. This was so he could help many people. But he had to interpret dreams to get him to the perfect will of God. Peter's purpose wasn't to be an evangelist, but to be an *Apostle* to help launch the first Church and many other congregations. But he had to operate as an evangelist in order to get to the perfect will of God. ***Note: A true apostle operates in all five ministry gifts when necessary.***

You must be doing it with no reservation.

Most of these people were already doing it

before the BIG event. Once they got to the big event, they were ready and prepared. David had already killed a lion and a bear before Goliath. Joshua proved his leadership skills before Moses died. Peter was already stepping up, taking charge, and showing his ability to be first before the day of Pentecost. Moses used his rod in the court of Pharaoh before the red sea. The widow woman was already cooking before the prophet came into her house. Joseph interpreted the dreams of two men years before he finally got the opportunity to stand before the most powerful man in the land- The Pharaoh. Doors will open for you when you're doing what you know to do at the right time. **God will never trust you with a big event if you're not active with what you have.** Preachers want national platforms, but they won't preach on the streets in their local community *(wanting a national platform is a bad motive anyway).* Singers and musicians want national platforms and big stages, but they won't <u>serve</u> in their local church on a small stage <u>**without getting PAID**</u>.

These people in the Bible I described changed the world in their lifetime. Will you change the world in your lifetime? Start thinking about your legacy. What are you doing now to prepare for the big event? It's always about what's in your hands. What has been dealt to you?

Proverbs 10:4 (KJV) He becometh poor that dealeth with a slack hand: but the hand of the diligent maketh rich.

Ecclesiastes 9:10 (KJV) Whatsoever thy hand findeth to do, do it with thy might; for there is no work, nor device, nor knowledge, nor wisdom, in the grave, whither thou goest.

Deuteronomy 2:7 (KJV) For the Lord thy God hath blessed thee in all the works of thy hand: he knoweth thy walking through this great wilderness: these forty years the Lord thy God hath been with thee; thou hast lacked nothing.

Chapter Nine
The Audacity of Breaking Out

Audacity: extraordinary boldness, courage

Joshua 1:6 Be strong and of a good courage: for unto this people shalt thou divide for an inheritance the land, which I sware unto their fathers to give them. 7Only be thou strong and very courageous, that thou mayest observe to do according to all the law, which Moses my servant commanded thee: turn not from it to the right hand or to the left, that thou mayest prosper whithersoever thou goest. 8 This book of the law shall not depart out of thy mouth; but thou shalt meditate therein day and night, that thou mayest observe to do according to all that is written therein: for then thou shalt make thy way prosperous, and then thou shalt have good success. 9 Have not I commanded thee? Be strong and of a good courage; be not afraid, neither be thou dismayed: for the Lord thy God is with thee whithersoever thou goest.

Joshua 14:10 And now, behold, the Lord hath kept me alive, as he said, these forty and five years, even since the Lord spake this word unto Moses, while the children of Israel wandered in the wilderness: and now, lo, I am this day fourscore and five years old. 11As yet I am as strong this day as I was in the day that Moses sent me: as my strength was then, even so is my strength now, for war, both to go out, and to come in. 12 Now therefore give me this mountain, whereof the Lord spake in that day; for thou heardest in that day how the Anakims were there, and that the cities were great and fenced: if so be the Lord will be with me, then I shall be able to drive them out, as the Lord said. 13 And Joshua blessed him and gave unto Caleb the son of Jephunneh Hebron for an inheritance. 14 Hebron therefore became the inheritance of Caleb the son of Jephunneh the Kenezite unto this day, because that he wholly followed the Lord God of Israel. 15 And the name of Hebron before was Kirjath–arba; which Arba was a great man among the Anakims. And the land had rest from war.

In 1983, the 61-year-old potato farmer won the inaugural Westfield Sydney to Melbourne Ultramarathon, a distance of 875 Kilometers (544 mi). The race was run between what were then Australia's two largest Westfield shopping centres: Westfield Parramatta, in Sydney, and Westfield Doncaster, in Melbourne. He ran at a slow loping pace and trailed the leaders for most of the first day, but by running while the others slept, he took the lead the first night and maintained it for the remainder of the race, eventually winning by ten hours. Before running the race, he told the press that he had previously run for two to three days straight rounding up sheep in gumboots. He claimed afterwards that during the race, he imagined that he was running after sheep and trying to outrun a storm. The Westfield run took him five days, 15 hours and four minutes, almost two days faster than the previous record for any run between Sydney and Melbourne. All six competitors who finished the race broke the previous record but were unable to match

Young's relentlessness and lack of rest.

Too many are doing what everyone else is doing. The majority is usually wrong. If everyone is doing it, do the opposite. Success starts with a willingness to break away from the crowd and do things differently. I once heard Peter Daniels say, he does things 40% better than anyone else. Therefore, he doesn't have competition. People who end up successful always goes against the grain. They do it differently than anyone else in their era. They pioneer the path for others. The have the audacity to break out. **They are bold in their pursuit to stand out and become specialists in their field.**

Numbers 13:17 And Moses sent them to spy out the land of Canaan **(Note: In business you need to know your competition and what you are facing. It's not to get fearful, but to see how to put together the right strategy. A person that doesn't spy is naive and will fail.)**, *and said unto them, Get you up this way southward, and go up into the* *mountain: 18 And see the land, what it is; and the people that dwelleth therein, whether they be strong or weak, few or many; 19 And what the land is that they dwell in, whether it be good or bad; and what cities they be that they dwell in, whether in tents, or in strong holds; 20 And what the land is, whether it be fat or lean, whether there be wood therein, or not. And be ye of good courage, and bring of the fruit of the land. Now the time was the time of the firstripe grapes. 21So they went up, and searched the land from the wilderness of Zin unto Rehob, as men come to Hamath. 22 And they ascended by the south, and came unto Hebron; where Ahiman, Sheshai, and Talmai, the children of Anak, were. (Now Hebron was built seven years before Zoan in Egypt.) 23 And they came unto the brook of Eshcol, and cut down from thence a branch with one cluster of grapes, and they bare it between two upon a staff; and they brought of the pomegranates, and of the figs. 24The place was called the brook Eshcol, because of the cluster of grapes which the children of Israel cut down from thence. 25 And* *they returned from searching of the land after forty days. 26 And they went and came to Moses, and to Aaron, and to all the congregation of the children of Israel, unto the wilderness of Paran, to Kadesh; and brought back word unto them, and unto all the congregation, and shewed them the fruit of the land. 27 And they told him, and said, We came unto the land whither thou sentest us, and surely it floweth with milk and honey; and this is the fruit of it. 28 Nevertheless the people be strong that dwell in the land, and the cities are walled, and very great: and moreover we saw the children of Anak there. 29 The Amalekites dwell in the land of the south: and the Hittites, and the Jebusites, and the Amorites, dwell in the mountains: and the Canaanites dwell by the sea, and by the coast of Jordan. 30 And Caleb stilled the people before Moses, and said**, Let us go up at once, and possess it; for we are well able to overcome it**. 31 But the men that went up with him said, We be not able to go up against the people; for they are stronger than we. 32 And they brought up an* *evil report of the land which they had searched unto the children of Israel, saying, The land, through which we have gone to search it, is a land that eateth up the inhabitants thereof; and all the people that we saw in it are men of a great stature. 33 And there we saw the giants, the sons of Anak, which come of the giants: and we were in our own sight as grasshoppers, and so we were in their sight.*

Caleb was bold. He had the audacity to speak differently than the others. He had faith in his mouth. The others were afraid and insecure. You don't have to talk and act like everyone else. Get bold and break out!

If you're going to break out, you must:

- Be willing to take persecution. You need tough skin. You will be rejected and laughed at.

- Be willing to be misunderstood.

- Be willing to be the only one excited about it.

- Be willing to be lonely. Pioneers are lonely.

- Be willing to go at it hard with limited resources, money, and support.

- Be willing to sacrifice more than ever.

- Be willing to communicate your vision consistently with enthusiasm.

Things you can do to go beyond the pack.

The average person does not plan, prepare, or make decisions based on future realities (vision). What you can do is have a yearly calendar. Here's why your calendar/to-do-list is so important:

- It sets priorities: for family, the Lord, and your business/job/schooling/minister

- It reflects your priorities: What you put on your calendar is what guides your time and life. Are you wasting your time and life?

- It determines your practices: Your calendar guides what you do and don't do.

- It maximizes your potential: It allows you to accomplish God's will and God's goals for your life.

Show me your calendar and check book and I'll show you what's important to you. ***What you're planning and buying is where your life will end up.***

People who go beyond the pack are bold investors. These investors invest into their brains. What are you reading? What are you learning in your field? What have you paid for lately that will help you get better?

You rarely do anything with a borrowed book-Peter Daniels.

You have a greater responsibility to things you invest into. Refuse to be an ignorant business owner, minister, volunteer in your church, or employee. Use your money to invest into your brain. **Go** beyond the crowd, **Ready** yourself for success through pursuit, and **Set** the tone for the next generation. Leave a legacy.

Chapter Ten

Don't Despise the "Going"

The *going* is like planting a seed. You go and things start out small and it looks insignificant. It's not insignificant but Satan and negative people want you to think that. That's just a trick of the enemy to divert you from having faith in God for the future (harvest).

Everything starts as a seed. You shouldn't despise the seed. You must start somewhere. This is why we are challenging you to GO first. Going means you at least have the ball rolling.

Zechariah 4:9 The hands of Zerubbabel have laid the foundation of this house, and his hands will complete it. Then you will know that the LORD of Hosts has sent me to you. 10 Do not despise these small beginnings, for the LORD rejoices to see the work begin, to see the plumb line in Zerubbabel's hand." (The seven lamps represent the eyes of the LORD that search all around the world.)

This literally refers to the building of the second temple, which was little in the eyes of many of the Jews themselves, who had seen the former temple; yet not in the eyes of the Lord of hosts, (Ezra 3:12) (Haggai 2:3 Haggai 2:6-9) and so we have the words,

``for who is he that despiseth this day, because the building is small?"

Ezra 3:11 And they sang responsively with praise and thanksgiving to the LORD: "For He is good; for His loving devotion upon Israel endures forever." Then all the people gave a great shout of praise to the LORD, because the foundation of the house of the LORD had been laid. 12 But many of the older priests, Levites, and family heads who had seen the first temple wept loudly when they saw the foundation of this temple. Still, many others shouted joyfully. 13 The people could not distinguish the shouts of joy from the sound of weeping, because the people were making so much noise. And the sound was heard from afar

As you can see the older Jews back then acted like most people today. *If it's small or if it starts out small, it literally gets despised.* The problem is they are going against God. And God is a God of increase, prosperity, big things, and growth. **He is also the God of small things, starts, new beginnings, and seeds.**

NEVER despise what God created and started!

Despise: *detest, hate, loathe, abhor, execrate, deplore, dislike*

There is too much despising of small beginnings (and small things period) and that is why many people won't step out and go. It is also why there is little to no GODLY increase. If there is increase while you're despising, it is happening because you're doing things in your flesh-on your own without God. You can prosper, increase, and have worldly success WITHOUT God.

If we despise where we are and if we're embarrassed, then we will be on our own *(using the latest secular strategies only to grow and increase)* **but there will be no glory and no peace.**

If you can't rejoice over a seed, you won't be rejoicing over a harvest. ***Despising small things is a sign of insecurity and immaturity.***

Seeds are small things that grow into larger things if they are properly nourished. Despising the seed is not nourishing it. **The seed is God's idea, so be careful how you treat it.** It's disrespectful to a pioneer when the people who are following are behind him/her despising and trying to rush things because they are feeling embarrassed.

Small is not a bad thing. Your mind as been trained to think if something just started and it's small, then something must be wrong with it. That's a deception. Some things start small and stay small and that still doesn't mean anything is wrong with it unless it is supposed to be big. The takeaway is: stop despising when things *start* and **stop despising small things period.**

Some of you may be struggling today because you have a bad case of despising. Despising is a heart thing and therefore you need heart surgery.

Increase will come and it is for due season, so stop being discouraged, embarrassed, and impatient. You know what's going to happen so work and wait on it. **<u>Despising will have you working without God.</u>**

- *Job 8:7 Though thy beginning was small, yet thy latter end should greatly increase.*

You'll never be a <u>GO.</u> Ready. Set. person if you despise small beginnings.

Be blessed – Doc Murphy

ABOUT THE AUTHOR

Doc Murphy is an apostolic leader, entrepreneur, and success coach known for igniting vision, faith, and movement in leaders across the nation. As founder of **The Everywhere Network**, **Everywhere Church**, and **Widman University**, Doc has dedicated his life to helping people discover purpose, walk in divine strategy, and build what God has placed in their spirit—without delay.

A dynamic speaker and business strategist, Doc teaches believers how to merge faith with action, vision with execution, and calling with results. His message is clear: *Potential means nothing without pursuit.*

From planting churches to building businesses, writing books, and mentoring next-generation pioneers, Doc Murphy continues to empower people everywhere to GO after the dream, get READY on the way, and watch God SET everything in motion.

Other Books and Products by Doc Murphy

Acceleration

<u>Deep Fake</u>

<u>MEGA Church</u>

YOU Success

Bridge Burners

Favor is Fair

J.O.Y.

Mature

Becoming The Balanced You

Dream Responsibly

Kingdompreneur

Everywhere University

The God of Increase

S.I. Supernatural Intelligence

Go Fishing

Five+One

The Authority of Kingdom Citizens

Personal Monetary System

Frequency

You are Exceptional

The Conqueror's Mentality

Defeating the Seven Enemies of Progress

#Everywhere

The Apostolic Church

Tent Makers

Rulers Of

Small Church Large Church

Christian Conduct

History Makers

Campfire

Prayer Protocols

Think Like the Boss

Rethinking and Redefining Honor

Leadership Lessons from John the Baptist

One Church Multiplied

Faith

How to get God to hear You

Holy Kiss

Full Time Believing

Pioneer Leaders

Worship Eps by Doc and Mariee Murphy and Everywhere Worship

Order these products @ amazon.com

A **MUST-READ:** *"ACCELERATION"*
BY DOC MURPHY

Go. Ready. Set.

Made in the USA
Coppell, TX
10 January 2026

68173904R00059